Doubtful Stamina

ISBN: 979-821-86316-6-6

Library of Congress Control Number 2025904380

Poetry by Jeffrey Hanson
Book design by Jill Flores

Published in association with
Village Books and Paper Dreams
1200 11th Street
Bellingham, WA 98225
villagebooks.com

Printed in the United States of America by IngramSpark

Doubtful Stamina

Poetry by
Jeffrey Hanson

VILLAGE BOOKS
—AND—
PAPER DREAMS
BUILDING COMMUNITY SINCE 1980

For you, Marilyn, my love and my life.

Contents

Dark Night

—for Mark Halliday

We know. He's a poet who presses flowers
Sweet Rhodora and Lady's Tress—
still white, still nodding.

And he's famous for saying: What's "good
for the soul is the work of the soul."
But no poem? No poem.

The storm knocks his door tonight.
Maples toss the dark wind from their leaves
while Walden's waters argue black and white.

Even so, muses must meet between page
and pen to tell us the beautiful thing.
We know.

What's "good for the soul is the work of the soul"
and a man makes "advances confidently in the
direction of his dreams."

But writing the beautiful and the pert is tough
and the storm pleads the worst of prospects
after all.

And prayer begs when the wrong god rules
and a poem about being without itself is nonsense.
So tonight, no begging. No god.

A sack of beans and a hoe in the corner are earthly
nodes that promise possibility. The cabin, the
hearth, the table and the lamp, the flame and the fire.

We know. To find the thing that must be found
the thing that makes the senses sing, the poet
must do battle.

We know he must stick close to possibilities
but raise a sword as well to abet the storm
that nudges nature to crack itself open, for us.

The Story Goes

There are certain themes I return to after I've
climbed the hill to see the other side: storms and
death, strife and survival, luck and second chances.

Over there, a bicycle rider and a cowboy inhabit
part of the view. The cyclist crouches crow-like as
if the road were prey. The cowboy slaps his steed
with familiar fluency.

A single tree, a massive oak, appears stoic and firm
before the coming storm that tears a stitch of sky
over the plain.

She can take it, that oak tree, rocking in place like a
star of the astrophysical sort, so rooted in the lyric
so steady against the changing times.

Of course, I have the liberty to place a barn on the
scene just as I like, one completely constructed
from my disease for speculation and fantasy.

A family of three hangs from a scorched rafter there.
I don't know why or what happened, but the
detail of shades that mark the barn door and the
ancient scent of blood, say enough about discord

and enough about decay, for me to know how the
story could go. That storm, though. That storm is no
figment of my making.

A bit too close to be far away, that storm is a bit too
graphic. Rain it will, come morning, for sure, and
later the riders will vanish while the oak will sense a
light spring snow.

The barn will burn down as a lie does when
questioned too much. Then not yet ready to walk
downhill, not finished sewing up the grim
particulars of the scene, I know how I'll strive and scheme.

The story of my fictional three in my fictional barn
will be revised as needed to set them walking up to
and over the next hill.

Moon Talk

Themes about the moon have tricked
people into blood feuds, gotten people
to sucking at late hours

kept people up, created legends of howling
people affected by the moon and
shot in the dark by a terrified farmer.

In various parts of the country, all affected
by the moon, affected by its evil light
people have pursed lips and wondered:

When will it stop its steady stare?
When it goes away, it reappears
unremittingly.

About the moon grandfathers say:
The moon is a thief, a fiery block-stone
whip-scarred bloom.

It curses with hope the unlucky.
Old men.
Unmoved haters of night.

For those emptied the moon is a pock
a silver sore, a scab of powder & ash.
The moon turns a blonde blue

and the moon sends a young man
to the cliffs on his twenty-eighth year.
Grandmothers soothe on moony nights.

To the children they say: It can't not hurt you no
ways. Blue moon is like the sea, blue like a hot
bright sky, chrome when you swing highest

and just when you nearly loop over, that joy
children, is moon blue. Real and not real
the moon must be silver, as honest as a coin.

Snow Blind

I try many things
carefully try them
as one might test
an untested weight
weighing

no strain
with purpose and care
with great care
the way one might
this early hour

try the neighbor's door.
But no, I don't do
anything really.
I stand here.
It's winter.

All has been done
about trees already.
The dark chatter of their forms
is cliché.
And sky and day?

What can be said?
White as a clockface.
When the time comes for snow
snow falls.
The first flakes sting.

So
I don't regret leaving
the rites of the season
to the season alone
to watch from my window

where the snow must score
its white sheet with words
at the back of my throat
to say nothing of the place
I turned to come home.

San Diego A. A.

I have a problem. I used to like to go to the park
drink a little wine but my life was lonely.
I begged God. I said to Him:

I know Father, you can save me. You can give me
what I need to make my life good, so I don't have to
moan to myself all the time, so I don't drink myself
sick anymore.

You can give me what I need, and I need a relationship.
I thought that was what I needed, someone to love.
Then like a miracle three days later up comes a
beautiful girl. A Mexican girl with long black hair.

She is only twenty-seven and I am an old man.
When I saw this, I said, Madre de Dios!
This I can't handle.

But she will not go away. I tell her so many times
Just go away. Please. You must go. But she stays.
I do not know what to do.

There is no sex. Nothing like that. She comes to my
house and showers, then goes to my bed. I sleep on
the couch. I have bad dreams. She is there, her face
like a vision

but this vision torments me. I worry all the time about her, where she is, what she is doing. It hurts me so I tell her she must leave.

What can I do? God has blessed me and cursed me too. I need a way out so I can be alone again but not kill myself and not drink anymore and not worry for a woman to make me happy.

One Road One Driver

Real roads are tactile
and mean something real

as a cold metallic wind
pours down from the hills.

Beneath the starlit
grids of heartache—

the color of rain-soaked
coal seams or the rent

away innards of consciousness—
is one road, one driver.

The stars tonight are silver mites
as a lanky awkward road raises its spine

with weight and purpose
to burden its shoulders

with the story of one who
snaps the radio to life

then lays on speed
because she cannot pray.

On Earth as It Is in Heaven

Once upon a time
Callie dozed at her food dish.

I was visiting from the city
but I could get country.

Past the white porch and screen door
hands up and passing over the table

hot rolls, buttered corn, drumsticks
and boiled yams.

Outside, thunderheads weltered.
Then, the winds blew hard.

The dust went flying over the okra.
The geese hid under the house.

A ladder fell from the roof as the oaks
howled, and the horses cut fast to the barn.

... kingdom come. Your will be done on
earth as it is in heaven.

While father said grace
no one looked up, but me.

Doubtful Stamina

October's off-season at Lake Jim
but whoever she was she was out
that day and naked.

Will and I were trying to see
just a little when the skiff
swamped fast.

Down went the motor, rods
and beer. It was goddamn cold
and we got near froze.

We were swimming like fetchers.
Then, Will cramped. "Jeff. S'gone!
Spooned up a demon!"

He yelled that to me like an old
Bible Hebrew. I could see he was blue.
How could he joke? The idiot.

And that's wide water south
then rain. I saw plain enough
how Will was fighting.

But how she was dreaming or a
hard sleep pinned her flat to the beach.
All that cold, she never moved.

When a stiff squall cut hard to the trees, they
leaned on their heels and chattered like static.
I beat it to shore but nearly drowned.

Retching and shaking, I knew right then.
Will, the poor bastard, was lost but
without a fault, as I knew him.

What'd he do as a mud-rotted goblin?
I wonder.
But no matter.

Now I think when danger eases and
summer returns, full alive but always
leaving, I'll still be a sucker.

Old Friend

Old friend, how do I explain how I've disliked you
for so long? Is there a way such news can be shared?
Maybe eye-to-eye, I might run you down with the
sheer force of my conviction to have *you*
apologizing to *me*.

Perhaps cheek-to-jowl in a long sad embrace.
"So long, my friend. Please forget me." Perhaps our
friendship might have thrived had we been separate
by circumstance. You shipwrecked on the Romantic
beach of Adventure and me waving briskly from the
shore across the channel, just to be nice.

I know I've been hateful, negligent, even
adversarial. For a way to share my regrets
we should talk, and I would, but ....
A lot of time has with it our names attached to
memory. For us there are plenty of links in the
chain of our conscription to "brotherhood."

If the pen is mightier than the sword or if it's about
right that written words can leave the poisoned pen
then believe I don't wish you violence or death.
But let this message make its way through me and
misplaced trust to get directly to the point.

Crossing the Line

All is not well. The mountain has claimed another hiker.

To deny oneself the safety of the track
to see a wisdom growing on the far hill
to swim in winter-chilled water, naked
and alone when all is not well, is to know
that you've crossed a line, willfully.
You feel it underfoot at the pond
where the beavers are.

The mud is extremely unsettling
a cold ooze, an aquatic slime
keeping company with the light rain
with the gray sky, and the fact that
you're broken and raw and ready.

Not lost, but idling undercover
to assert your resolve to stray
to decenter, to imagine yourself
as a scatter of bones, a nest of hair.

What's In a Name

"If the names are unknown knowledge of the things also perishes"
        —*Linnaeus.*
Nassarius Gibbosulus: snail shells used as ornaments 70,000 years ago.

We'll call him Lewis
the one who resembles so many.
In our memory, there he is
calling his dogs, Adam and Eve.

That's Lewis. I know Lewis.
Lewis has had powerful moments.
He once punched Paul for mashing Marge.
All night after, Lewis & Marge.

It may be the name Lewis
is too modest for our species.
But Maynard's a boob, Victor's snide
and Grenville's a bit fancy for our tastes.

Come here, Lewis, I say
while the night's black
and the stars are boiling.
Let's get drunk and listen to Jerry Lee.

I don't drink anymore
he replies, in his friendly way.
You know, Lewis, I've been thinking.
I might stop drinking, too.

Then I see him stoop to pick up a stone
squinting to get a good look.
Sounds like a good idea to me, he says
but what can we do about this?

Lewis has found a tiny shell very old
and from God knows where.
Nassarius Gibbosulus, says Lewis
looking quite pleased with himself.

Come Glory

In glory, we rise
and in bliss—our bodies

we shed. Worry obsolete
death, laughter, dread.

Who is spared
when a culling grows?

Nimbus blooms are we
lest the Gardener lifts our heads.

Then, we're through.

Excellent Potential

We'll buy everything.
Say cuss-words in church
And dream a dream we don't deserve
Just to be that couple.

And like we're lucky-lucky
We'll run up on the world
Change it, make it all again
Or beat it down with glamour.

Come smoke & ginger
Say that watercolor thing
So fine we're nearly ugly
So fine we dance in mineral light.

Are we perfect?
Strong and sour
When no one ever is?
Everyone is saying

We get to be the alphabet.
We get to own religion
Like a comb
Or like our very favorite thing.

When I Went to Work

At 18 I became a ditch digger and meant to show
the old men who hired me that I had iron.
The first day I jumped on it. Never stopped.
The day-help got pissed and told me
They pay by the hour, man.

When I busted curb & gutter with a 90-pound jack
I slammed into it all day.
While the sun raked a fire across my back
I filled the dump truck, filthy.
I had heart. I could take it.

When I got to the trades at 23
I laid 12 squares in 8 and knew my shit
drove nails all day, wore a straw hat
bandana, nail pouch, and boots.
The universe and I were tuned-up and wired.

Cover that zipper, then lay up the gravy.
It's all straight-go on the gables
but you gotta slow down on the rakes.
I showed new guys how to pour it on.
They saw how I loved to punish myself.

But tender dusks at quitting time made a poet of me.
It was the same whenever we stood near the trucks
to smoke and drink though I never let on.
Quiet eyes and small talk turned up a rock inside as
the weepy old woman I am would start pinching at
the lump in my throat.

The Sell

Whitefield Cosmetic's Lily Greasecomb
set up shop in Silo, California
at the El Sol Motel
to sell the wives some makeup.

While their earthmen worked the fields
they joined in a lot under a tree.
There was a card table and paper tablecloth
and on that table was makeup.

Lily used her words carefully.
With spatial gestures
she split her speech
using still verbs and hissing syllables.

Soon Lily had them wearing lipstick
called Hot Hearts.
Looking like ghosts, they danced to records
with a thick gleam above each eye.

Gifts

Think again, lovers. Love Love.

The little stars have sent
the purest light God has for us

have every night shellacked a hard light
a difficult light
over mosques and churchyards

Love Love
and love being loved.

With every breath, believe.

Faith and love
you will one day send to Night
who does not need
anyone.

Volunteers

There needed be gardens at our big church.
There needed be beauty made risen from nothing:
new sod and roses, planters set straight, a lime
three figs and commonsense taste about statuary.

Our church where we meet had a plain need for
perfect.
Lilies too. So, it was.

We scoured the soil clean of its weeds.
For Him, my son, my husband, and I
made glory bear witness for grace.

There needed be gardens, and so it was.
There needed be glory for God-glory there.

No friend could pass and not see what we did
how we offered to gladden, to amend our world
to let it shine for the Gardener, our God
who tears at the bramble and cuts the wild vine.

Service

They approach
out from the afternoon rain.
Bible-thumpers.

Rain dogs bark
and gray doves fly.
Is this church?

The gray sky.
Two clocks cluck.
Black dress-shoes V'd

and Bible books kneed
up and open.
Suits and ties.

Have you prayed for our visit?
Oh, yes, I have.
I've been praying like a drunkard.

Time and Tide

The time reels forward as fish do, whirling and
banking through glaucous waters offshore

and you've come to spend the latter part of day
investigating every speck of sky in slow float over the sea.

There's Kevin and William.
Their voices shred fast and flap off with the wind

down the long trail of salt sputum.
The single line between sea and sky is holding.

Such a thing is the clock that pounds out hours
in waves and spray.

No one's ever more alone
than while being alone with the sea

with the wind that won't cease
laying its pulse to the ear in odd time

as urgent and persistent as the sea-lost who slap
with opened hands windows on rescue.

The Magnificent Ninety

There were only ninety, I said.
This, the argument between us.

Caravels! I yelled.
Our bedroom deadened the word.

Small Portuguese venture-ships
designed to discover new trade routes, honey.

What ninety men would challenge those seas?
Around the Cape to Asia!

Ninety men
The small caravels

Those ships were Portuguese venture-ships, babe
meant to chart every inlet and shore, but *so* small.

Prince Henry sent them beyond the bulging Cape.
Maybe to their deaths!

When they returned traders sent them farther.
What did anyone care for sailors? She undressed.

Ninety men Small Caravels

Ninety men Small Caravels
Ninety men Small Caravels

"You're drunk. Get to bed," she said.
Portuguese voyagers though.

I sat on the bed, staring. Cape Bojador.
What could I do but wait for morning?

I knew I'd feel smug at first light, private and cold.
Then behind my eyes, like a sneeze coming on

pity pushed up a monumental mood.
Brother, I said to the dark and meant it.

Civilization (I See a Train)

My imagining places me there.
Pines loom through fog.
A chrome moon says cocktails.

Here they are:
cart, white linen
silver salver, neat drinks.

Ah, yes.
Civilization.
But where are you?

Where are you, dear?
You. You. You.
Far below the cliffs

the sea keeps reaching.
How easy to keep reaching
when the heart is memory.

Yesterday reminds me
Don't go too far, Jeff.
Where must we end?

How do we face the cold lands
to depart for the gravel
and grizzly slush of home?

Good Questions

No one has asked me
to keep them in mind

or asked me to burden
myself blood and soul.

But sleepless nights
it's just me asking

alone, anxious
contrite.

Do you know what I ask
as I look up to silence?

Then you know what I know
unless you've stopped asking.

The questions themselves
unanswered

and handwringing
mollify, a little.

Penal Drift

I dreamed us a get-away, Will, a goddamned goody
to fly with a mermaiden bowsprit bare bust-to-bowels
blue skin to scales, on the gouge of a vision boat.

I dreamed us a woman aboard our No 'Rythmetic
Will. When doldrums starch flat a running black sea
and the moon claps a fog to its watery eye, we'll be
swinging, drunk, and alive.

I dreamed us as thieves of that woman, Will, who'd
once asked for better but fell on her tempers to ride
red wishes like a wild fool. In the French, we'll
name her Drowned Fool.

Let's play the whole stage of it, Will, and see it full
volume: bark chips of islands on the soft chalks of
dusk. The blue milks of wakes boiling off into history.

And we'll have him too, Punch Lucky.
He, we'll name Man and haul him 'cross the
pumpkin reef. And you, Will, can hold over hard
on that genesis of sins, the human heart.

But for me to strike fresh, our two-fisted boilers
must knuckle down and blow to the stars
a bone-quaking blast to have each of us tasting
the smoke we'll ride.

Woman will choose what the water buries and
you, if you like, can drown yourself, Will, but I see
myself playing smart for the century, riding the
spillers and making way fast for the first last vestige
of decency.

Fresh Haircut

Even before the first doubt, your story has begun.
The engine's shot. You're out of the car
turning in place, hand cupped over your eyes

and you see the sun, high and white, and the far-off
mountains bunched at the desert's edge.
But you won't see what you hope to see.
No one comes so far.

Before you realize how close you are to the drop
the brakes have stopped smoking. All the way down
an old wreck, a fifties-something.

You spend a few minutes deep breathing lots of warm
dry air and you notice it all to be lit so fine.
It feels great to be alive.

The light on your feet, and the warmth those feet
feel firmly affixed to the sand. It's too much.
It's wonderful.

But there are doubts to address.
You're alone, can't wake up, can't cheat.
No one's going to bail you out or give you their best advice.

The wind that won't stop blowing knows how to chill you
and how to rattle the creosote, and who will know if you
turn to salt to blow away and over the arroyos?

Today, you want to discover you're made of iron
and this'll be a great one to tell anytime.
There's a long walk ahead as afternoon's slipping fast.

This is good, this story of yours.
Don't worry about its meaning though. Really.
You're the fresh haircut and new sandals

and the day is yours and the night as well
when star-grit will shimmer the void overhead
this time just for you. For you, right? Right.

Fruit Fall

Above, clouds on the mountain.
Below, fruit-spoil and deep sun
simmering in a veil of haze
and glare outright on the river.

Its sprained flux lies exhausted
and afloat in small pools glazed
with mercurial light.
Everything is green.

Every bit of matter is green or night
or it is the ceaseless strafe of heat
from the sun baking the skin.
Ashanti, Kirabu, or Eve, we can't know.

What does it matter?
Across grass and the flint pit she comes
freighting fruit fall in her pungent arms
and with her the cool, cool, rain.

Night Light

It's this day again and I
choose to keep it near tonight

to slip through bad dreams
as yellow day glazes
my shoulder with light.

I'll peer with contempt
at the red razor-slice
at the bruise blue strangulation.

And as new days meet
all the days I have known
I'll relish their powers to sustain.

I'll choose to believe the verdant
jolt of tomorrow's fertile promise
and then

when night threatens again
I'll beg it mercy for my trying
to do the impossible.

For trying to escape with light
up the well from my just deserts.

Damage Control

If you are alone, washing a few dishes, and it's
winter, it's night, and you see your son's image
floating at the window in a cold light, then that is no
visitation or sign of his spirit flying back to check on you.

He's gone, but not dead. He lives with his mother in
Crete, too young to be any more than a ghost to
you—your far-away son, his face like a little moon
like a photograph.

And now his mother has her son and her voice has
placed a tonnage on you. You don't answer the
phone, but the messages get through: irresponsible
asshole self-absorption fake.

How can I advise you for healing? Phaedra is your
third wife, Adam, your second child. I say the child
is gone. Be alone.

I've told you what to do:

Walk through your new town—a long, long ways—
until it runs out to flat fields. Believe me, Will, I see
you, the old Will, standing like a hero, a few clouds
shredding out high overhead. It's cold and windy so
everywhere there is an icy burning, but the vision is warm.

The new man says: I can lose this child to survive.
I can find my love and leave it here, and get to my
worst. I can walk home strong and new and finally
ruthless.

I've said, if you can't get moving, lock up tight and
eat a mountain of food: half a dozen eggs, brauts,
a few beers, and fat white potatoes, fried hot.

In the quiet, the skull eats, the eyes see nothing, the
hand forks up what you've made. And all this will
put you down into a suffocating sleep where life is a
line of light breath, and that's all.

You'll heal if you wait until your boy can suffer
until he's old enough to feel what damage is
waiting. See what distance does now? Nothing.

Out there, boys will learn to walk and talk before
they wonder what they are, before they know how
to measure fathers with their own ideas about absence.

Slow Dissolve

The sun boils down into the hills.
Wines and lavenders of evening.

The clutter of land grows less delicate
then nearly at once it is simple with

lines of dark forms on soft braille.
Stars turn out individually on time

as the breeze rings a clean quiet
through uncountable grasses.

There's no story, Mother, no sense
except the warps and flurries of time

or the swelling vacancy
I call confusion from which

I can't stop hoping to sense
a single first clear word.

Late Walk

big red truck green grass
white farmhouse

cutting between the hills a robin's-egg blue
a man must lean on his liquor

getting through the prayer line
walking fields with all colors

flaring soft or fired with hard light
the walnut shell his face is

the tan smeared greasy eyes
a mature man out of time

behind that pretty wandering
through shreds of veiling clouds

beyond the altitudes
a whole empty country

tough cut grass hard brown boots
bigger sky each swallow

The Church Where I Go Has No Idols

They were removed and sold
said a plaque, sometime in nineteen-twelve.

"We have heaven and ourselves"
I was told by Brother Rowland

one summer night under the arch
of the open door.

"What do we need with marble doodads?"
he asked, in fun.

"That's for Christendom, the old
 garlanded whore. For you, I have a hand"

which he presented.
"The hand that gives, gathers."

Then, I think he would have winked
had we not caught the possible impropriety.

Enough North

Far enough north, the growing of our good
land of earning stops as a final tide.
There we enter strong enough, strong enough
to purchase pride and will from our lacking.

And that man that woman that child are the
suffering signs we must suffer.
Their circumstance has wrought them so burning
a blaze from which we run to our fires hot and calm.

We move no farther north than what marks our full
resolve to step a notch toward that country of winds.
Where are the temperatures for swimming? And the
green grasses of hot hues? The warm sands
underfoot, in our own lands?

Instead, we chop-block the lens of glass waters at
our feet and build our homes of water where each
has a hole for coming and going and for watching
the shades that flutter the mile where the south will
also be soon to close in.

Purple Passage

Say we cover the child ourselves with starlight
with manufactured fictions of plenty.

Consider quacking bells of pain
drown under negation by will.

Jesus, did I just write that?
I mean, say we accept death

or church becomes the place we stay
with an oak out front and a man walking by

hot summer day, a swift's tail jutting from
the eaves, a radio drowsing in the scriptorium.

Oh, my God! Is it okay?
What I mean is

we are and then we aren't
and then we are again.

That's what I mean
and these words are little prayer flags.

Valentine's

I see that lovers at windows evoke
an essence of breath and brick
of frame and oil.

I see the red hearts on napkins
puffed with color shining up like apples
and a whisper creaks within.

I have seen it in cafes
with whirling wood-blade fans
fluttering above our little group.

I have seen it at Valentine's
when I looked down under my glass
where water cuts tissue and again that creak.

Sally

Sunburned and drunk
he sprawls wet and winded.

The boats are out
and she's on the Sally.

She's thin, she's brown
and her feet are long

but her hair when it's wet
couldn't be better.

Heat grips him:
orange fireballs behind the lids

droplets dribble to dry
his scalp itches.

As her lotion rides the breeze
he lies still as stone.

He'll never chance disdain.
He's now inert, replete

and as patent as
a lump of ore.

"Send for me, Sally.
I won't come.

But if you spoke
what would you say?"

First Thing, First Light

Lie with day over your cotton covers:
Like flame-light it burns the cold away
And the sun, like a peeled orange, hovers
At "your chill bumped shoulder," the poets say.

It's warm down there where your fingers play
At keeping it simple. The primal heart
Draws up, inflates and tenders a spray
Of pictures from where your red passions start.

Then stars burn clear as the thick oceans part
Out from the dark bones of a private world.
A warm air orbits where the covers dart
Then blows like hell when the flags unfurl.

Ignoring the ritual coffee's black murk
Say "I will, I do" to your handiwork.

About Boys Jumping

About boys jumping, I can attest.
I can say the lake one day
hooked so closely to the sky
that both became the same blue.

And like a memory of rapture
joy broke through.
Those boys jumped high, flew and fell
completely into the lap of day.

Looking up from the water one could
see the other walking his feet mid-air
then escaping to shore, climbing
the risk and then falling again.

And all of it laughing and hoarse yelling.
Too high, of course. Too high.
But no one could see the picture they
made of themselves breaking rules

testing their powers as if commanded
while beyond the hills and wild trees others
could not know what the boys were that day
except for other boys like those.

Beach Book Romance

Breakers sign the sand
and I see feet

yours tanned
mine white.

And here we are
emerald surf, aqua wind

a white-light smudge
of clouds at the brim

your floral letterbox
and gold pen

sea-sky and shimmer
maybe rain.

Beside us, Chester
and Dearie doze dazed.

"We *will* love"
our dialogue asserts.

Down the beach
a happy old couple.

He, potbellied
bronzed.

She, like a hare
fit for the spit.

Both are muscled
grizzled, athletic.

As you turn the page
I pour from the flask

while in my brain
I dare proclaim:

"Our world is not fiction.
Sunset's cliché

of today's final hour marks
the place we *will* get to."

Believing the Difference Matters

I haven't yet had my idea of life spoiled by serious illness. Perhaps this is a stupid statement, but the thought seemed logical and poetic as I drove home from work late this afternoon and saw all the old things in a different way.

Fall maples flared more intensely in the six o`clock sun while oncoming cars glowed their colors like candies. And the pass between Athens and The Plains—once a graceful hill blown out to make a road when I was maybe twenty and living in California—reformed its ancient ridge whole again.

How would I have known as a young man that I'd see those rock walls at forty-six under a clear sky and think of dying? Mortality can't ruin an evening like the one I had planned tonight.

But tonight is different too. There's a quarter moon in a black sky over my yard. It floats; it appears fresh-washed; it's high and cold and says to me something difficult I know about myself. I've been trying to fool a dying friend.

She has so much cancer it's unseemly. It's wrong for
me to see it like this. Her blood is filthy with
disease and maybe because I'm scared, it's all right
for me to be haunted and disgusted too by her
struggle to move through her house, point by point,
from the sofa to the bathroom to the bedroom,
bravely floating her strengths above the gravity of
these dangerous days in a world that will bury her, sure.

Because I've seen it before in another friend twenty
years ago, I know when someone dies slowly this
way, the animal keeps kicking. People see it as
fighting to live, but it seems purely organic, to me.
That animal won't stop beating the bars until it has
pulverized the will to run. And then, when the
personality remembers its old perfect honesty
everything familiar drops beyond humor and
complexities into a hole.

Well, hypocrisy, in this case, is kind and does some
good over the phone when I pretend. I fool myself
to be earnest. Maybe what I want will swim up from
the dark. I want it to surprise me.

But phrasing up hope seems a sort of necessary
stupidity. I say the things I wish for because I love;
love exists and must be rewarded, sometimes. And
if there's love, there's beauty. And then, of course,
I must believe in the beauty I felt this afternoon.
I would go crazy otherwise.

But this belief is similar to what I learned as a kid
cutting school, then sneaking up to watch how
things were unchanged by my mischief. It hurts, but
the strange misery of it felt like growing up and
understanding what no one can say.

Maybe having faith means believing in what it is I
like to think, that our best hope is to look ahead
without fear. To accept what can't be changed.
After all, who knows what good will come from
future dangers or how blessed we'll be someday to die.

What Can You Do with a Drunken Sailor?

You might want to take him home.
Early morning, in your kitchen

there he'd be.
Simple as that.

He's handsome. Right?
He makes you laugh without even trying.

Maybe he could tune your guitar
or get the car running again.

Squinting at the sunrise, cocking his head.
Jesus, you need this.

But there's something about travel in how he
stubs a cigarette into your mother's good cup.

You know, don't you?
A fire burns at the root of his thirst.

In the end, he'll only get drunk, fall down
and sleep, just as pleased as a little baby.

At Big Palm

At Big Palm—new things.
For Dale, an item of clothing (a silk-something for
the neck), a chest of diaphanous scarves, a pin.

Smith receives the good graces of Salena.
Claudia enjoys a reprieve while the scene
illuminates privately.

Greta now owns a little man on which to impose her
obsessions for wild living.
All are equals, yet each is different from the others.

Then, table set, bright sunlight clocks across the
room, through the blinds. Exegesis is not needed
nor are such fussy assessments missed.

Everything pauses and pulls ahead, in kind, as the
story proceeds like the strong pulse traveling head
to foot in a healthy child.

The friends seem eager to think of something to do
for which they will later be condemned by those
who gnash their teeth and spit fire.

Three proclaim how the nude confirms our will to
counter convention, to see into a yellow sun, to feel
pleasure under the gray cast of rain showers.

A blessing and jewelry are exchanged behind the
shadow of the kitchen wall. A spaniel trots past
before disappearing the rest of the day into another room.

Paul arrives to surprise everyone.
Could any of them not agree that he is the best-looking
man any have ever seen?

No one becomes jealous, however, because Paul's
gifts allow him to charm all alike, so the group
predictably yields to his advantage.

While Sissy sits fireside, William hangs his latest over
the mantle; a blue canvas, a furious sky, and someone
rowing out and away and over the chop and into the
grip of a livid sea to appear here as D.

Let's Be Young Again

I know
open places

bright black
nights

falls
cold gravel

the snap-snap of lips
to the ear.

Beautiful
confidants.

Soon, it's late.
We forget.

You are out here.
You approve.

I say, A cold,
lonesome place

high and cool
the moon.

You?
Oh, you say

Come.
I've a secret.

High Language

Perfection is the perfect word, with denotations of
excellence strung 'round her like disciples. She
studies with ease eyes that study her. She bears her
breast to the finger that points. Oh yes, word of words.

Orgasm or rapture she sums up textually
verbally and cerebrally. How grand an ideal this
queen of ideals who sits on the page, imperial
brave, and unburdened by expectations of those
who seek so much of She who says it all.

A little pronoun like me must be overruled by how
many, dullard, work-a-day nouns? And with the
logic of unimpeachable ranking, those nouns each
day address the world while wearing their variant
gowns for use that God has pressed into service.
Look.

The language of things makes its mark on a world
adorned with flair and an abundance of attendant
adjectives. And when the spectacle of signs proves
too much, those most useful of utilities must be
dismantled and warehoused as the mumbling mind
purges all the inky stains of seeing.

The whole population of print can be clapped shut
and silenced at the back pocket of oblivion. But
who doesn't know how the prayer arrives on the
tongue of each hour? Driving alone, cutting the
meal into pan-sized portions, even getting up
quietly to pee at night or any old thing done anytime.

No words will matter, and no forms can manage the
graphic of apprehensions at work in the blood. Not
being perfect ourselves, we've done the best we
can, and something like our efforts to live well is
synonymous with the word *absolution*.

Something Approaches Unknown

because this something is vague.

It comes to mind as a small servant to do what must
be done:
    arrange heavy blooms at the broad white
    windows; set astir the room's labor of
    antiquity; remove with care wax paper from
    a sweet cold sandwich.

These things even a vague outline of something can do:
    the house becomes the heart, and the wind
    hears it calling; no language but a blot of
    starlings spurts crossways over the road
    calamitous gesture of shape and no-shape of
    flash and fog.

Negation becomes a furrow of plenty where nothing is a
white flourish:
    the great warm violence of summer
    the rain-shimmer of the table knife
    a call to service from a need to serve.

Universals Aside

Time is a River
the Heart, a Lion

grooming red paws
when sated

and Memory cheats
as Memory will

while Truth explains
It is what it was, man.

Faith proclaims: I am
Faith who sees the Light

And Death is he
who sweeps the dust

while rain or no rain
the Sun peeks from the hill.

His gaze is youthful
sweet and winning

and such delicious
optimism.

Body Language

To acknowledge loss is good, a sort of painful ownership
that comes with maturity. But to do so means
I must take a moment to be quiet, out of respect
to stop talking, to let the charge of my pulse speak for me.

I can see how the clouds are always "saying" without words
dark on gray for rain or wind-scrubbed white and blown
over blue like seafoam skipping airborne over sand.
Fit signs for how we lose the present to the future ahead.

Perhaps you might join me. I see you there, off a little way
standing motionless while looking toward the waves
pretending not to notice how lonely I seem at my end
of this deserted place.

I can't know if you want to walk down my way for a word.
But I gather from your body language that I do appear
lonely to you and that maybe you understand how my
heart's the nuisance I own which needs a little quiet
before good company stops to say "Hello."

Tools

Put them away. Keep tools clean
with new grease like brass-honey
oilcloth, box, and shelter.

Take care to use each for the other
so the whole adheres to ideas of
policy and procedure.

Make each tool beautiful, as perfect
as a photograph that renders the
pleasure of permanence so well.

Then they will remain as they should remain
outlasting the maker while showing the worker
what a worker can do with good clean tools.

About keeping things right, the grandparents say:
You can always change plans when the tools
are ready. Right as right, they say, True as true.

Come

My friends, I invite you.
Join me beneath a summer shower
at Kachelmacher Park.
Please, no gift.

Bring Ramey, Cloe, and Stuart.
Strong, warm, and young.
They laugh about everything.
Else, we'll need alcohol.

I've gotten a bike, so I'll ride it
even through the rain.
I'm still smoking.
Don't judge.

When we meet, I'm likely to play cool
killing the *this* in me for *that*.
The blues will make a slow-swirl inside
but that's just fine, I suspect.

Little Poem

I will place you in a drawer
Just as you are, like this
To my right

This drawer
Unmissed, my darling
Uncalled

And so like the so-what
Of everything so perfect
Without you.

A Poem About Athens Ohio

The prophet says:
"Town, small city, biograph.
People on the plain near the river.
Rain tells its story of blind purpose.
The wind will blow."

We say:
"As town and people
we are the family names of places we belong
and we are strong.
Make us good citizens even when eyes
are dulled and dreamy and we forget."

Tonight:
red singe of sundown, fleeing.
Lamp-lit shop for leather, flowers
bells, and buddhas, brickwork streets
the pacific, open, college green
seized in place at the bell tower.

Here:
good Athenians, we examine our lives.
We commend our prophets and our profs.
We do everything, in Athens.

We write and read and sing.
We cry and spread our hands wide to beg.
We confess and with our eyes we love out loud.

On the Hocking:
river trees tug at the world.
Their living greed for life
knots and fidgets underground.
They look like trouble when storms come.
Tonight, they are what the land says.

I say:
"Democracies of spirit make us all politicians.
Festivals, celebrations, great events.
Causeways reach toward where the road urges.
Athenians, everywhere, be yourselves!"

As you can see:
I've started placing pictures in my poems.

Free-spirited, love-loving citizen, mine
I know what you'll do
next time we meet at Donkey.
Placing an Americano back on the table
you'll say:
"Do what you like, man. It's cool."

I Am Going to Write

I am going to write
so I must not lie
saying here the sky's
not good enough
or the ground
not ready for blood.

But thing of wheels whipping
I will write
or cottonmouth blacktop
flowers of cumulus
smokes on the sky.

At the table
I write.
I am at least a fool.

The window here gets
fit for its burden of daylights
for cratering sun-falls, again.
That's good.
Black. White.
Writing makes me sick.

But I go like a guy
heading to sea, slow-stride
with courage
jumping off the chest bone.
I'm wanting, goddammit
to be beautiful.

Acknowledgements

I would like to gratefully acknowledge the following publications where these poems have previously been published:

34th Parallel
    Beach Book Romance

Amethyst Review
    Dark Night

Bangalore Review
    Late Walk

Blood Orange
    Damage Control
    San Diego A. A

Blue Collar Review
    When I Went to Work

Forge
    Believing the Difference Matters
    Doubtful Stamina

Paper Salad
    Moon Talk

Poetry Pacific
    Time and Tide

Riverwind
Snow Blind
What Can You Do with a Drunken Sailor?

The Adroit Journal
Excellent Potential

The Laurel Review
Body Language
High Language
Purple Passage
Something Approaches Unknown

The New Indicator
The Sell